SLUR OUEVRE

JAMES D'AGOSTINO

SLUR OUEVRE

JAMES D'AGOSTINO

NEW MICHIGAN PRESS
TUCSON, ARIZONA

NEW MICHIGAN PRESS
DEPT OF ENGLISH, P. O. BOX 210067
UNIVERSITY OF ARIZONA
TUCSON, AZ 85721-0067

<http://newmichiganpress.com/nmp>

Orders and queries to nmp@thediagram.com.

Copyright © 2011 by James D'Agostino.
All rights reserved.

ISBN 978-1-934832-29-5. FIRST PRINTING.

Printed in the United States of America.

Design by Ander Monson.

Cover image "First Words: Ouch" — copyright Aaron Fine.

CONTENTS

Among the Attributes of a Basically Cruel Man   1
Repair in All Its Branches   3
Kaboom Aubade   5
Mar   6
Iron-Clad Lullaby   8
Kum & Go Mirror   10
Penultimatum   11
Sole Eve Speaker Adam Spoken to Eve   13
On the Long Standing Relationship Between
    the Fingersnap and the Words *Like That*   15
Transcendental Anchorage   18
No Note   20
Mine Own Recognizance   21
Weathermanic   22
Listing   24
Survival of the Fitting   27
Minimum Security Blanket   29
How to Hand Scissors or Knives to Someone
    You Like   31
Cincinnatia   33
River as a Rain Museum   35
Ardor Vitae   38
Black Tern   40
Echo Local   42

Deus Ex Mackinaw   45
The Boy and the River Between the Girl
    and the Sea   47
Slide Guitar Sunday   50
Notable Captures   52
In Command of Irregulars   53
What I Always Thought I Taught This Town's Sons
    About Its Daughters   55
Tuesday Co-Ed Minor Champions   57

Acknowledgments   61

For Dean Young, and again, for Karen

It's not that an applied layer of gentleness is respected and admired most among the attributes of a basically cruel man. It's that the average person, which you are not, and I am not, is fooled by it.

—Edna Ferber
in a letter to James Dean

AMONG THE ATTRIBUTES
OF A BASICALLY CRUEL MAN

Today began a dreamsicle
made of dirt and up to us
to pilot this sky's specific
dye lot. And why not?

Our lives are six or seven
people a lot, a couple dozen
less so, and an even call it
hundred lesser still. Today

it's the cinnamon blush
of rust on a dumpster.
It's the city's talc of salt
and still ice bites onto the lot

in a couple spots. Took the skull
for a crawl is all and tried not to
fall through a city ultimately
solvable, mere matter

of form. The locksmith's truck
fits surely into traffic. I've
climbed through four windows
twelve times, emerged smudged

or scraped, but home, where
the thing about charm's it
doesn't give a fuck what
comes after adoration, only

more and more.

REPAIR IN ALL ITS BRANCHES

I was born, but couldn't
leave it there.
                Every shoulder I'd slobbered over after seemed okay

with it. Shadow seemed more cut and dry, but shade
just seemed confused and grew
                        my fondness for epistolary cry.

Someone was always moving one step ahead or behind. O,

I were perfect and kind
                of tried to make my best impression
on any pillow I encountered. It's the only

thing I know how to make.
These poems aren't made.
                  These poems are about afternoon,
nice guy, stray dog, dark
              with god, thick with
waffles, and when a character

enters, he enters in the costume of the imaginary

man, a perfect fit, even
the snag in the sleeve, even

in ice-thin New Year's light that makes maples into
birches

and birches into lightning
in storage.
        Truest thing I could stand was
on my porch, snap off icicles and toss them
to the stairs to hear the shatter.

KABOOM AUBADE

Other things can flaunt their not being
here—you, for instance, me. Our sky
just a blood orange-borne dinge

and I'm doing it again. You can't stand me
saying sunset's candy anymore, ditto
children's aspirin, and I keep telling

you, baby, you're thinking of dawn,
you got me all wrong. Twenty good
seconds of it, February rain,

and after cars on wet streets
rub it all over themselves loudly. Late
morning and the day seems already

under-blundered, everything exactly
where it could be. Let's just see
what we can't do about that.

MAR

I'm still misspelling March,
but at least it's not harm.
At least it's charm. I am

hoping for ham soon. I am.
At this point the only reason
I can conceive of even going

to the gym is I kind of someday
want to do coke. Back home
I've got parts of one or two

poems if I'm lucky and parts
of lots if not. First fly of the year
slow to my swat, but so what it

had only half my heart. If that
is the first switch of Summer
flipped, fine, but if it can't

last the night, if this is just
the crumbs of hundreds down
here in the noun-scrounge

I want out. I can't man
the cram cam. I can't.
There's already something

you told me to remember
I forgot, but that's what
made it, you say, so.

IRON-CLAD LULLABY

I've often tried to figure out why,
without looking it up
because that would be too easy,
the world is not a book.
Rain in sheets, itself
an ink, all squall
until instantly it stills,
steams in the street
once the sun
picks back up where it
last left off. Just north
of Bachelor, exit 155
leads east to the Missouri Girls Town
and west toward Nostalgiaville.
So again life's laid right out
with a highway down its spine,
making this 2-way stop its middle
age, and Nostalgia, an algae
occluding ponds some are fond of
finding time to skate on and later
remember about 85% of,
so more and more clouds
are pressed into absent mountain
service, and that
stands in for this,
the way cotton blown

across the road makes due
with Michigan winters
merely remembered.

KUM & GO MIRROR

Here in the risen column of asparagus
piss vapor somewhere near Keokuk,
IA, I swear if I knew where

to hide you I'd kill you. Outside in
the crawlspace of the sky, I decide no
more last year open pit of ash and gasoline

in between what seemed me and everything
and get in. The road's alright. It rained hard
all day just not here. A clump of maples

hoist last handfuls of light until a few
final leaves figure out how to glow then
it's gone, and the cloud scraps lit apricots

that got a minute, tops, to get gawked at,
dropped into a sonnet and sealed up good.

PENULTIMATUM

Down here on the business end of the very beginning,
either I'd either X or Y or it was over. *There are no*

corrections or clarifications today. Says so, right
there, page one, below the fold. Behold: another

perfect yesterday for the *Post Intelligencer*. So maybe
every mayor's name remains unmolested, and each

face free to exude its truths in these duly proofed
depictions of an ordinary Saturday. I figure February

maybe never ends. Almost every afternoon ever
encoded by birdsong into contemporaneity comes

to and comes to this. A guy pries siding off
the less and less light blue house across from us—

me and my her, she and her what's his face.
Though I'd thus and suched through much of us,

we really were an outgoing message. It's a real
sweet song, *Help Me*, and there's many. There

were big things and there were little things and
always it was possible to fall between, unsound

as the footing seemed, waking to my stake in it,
the heart. From the wrong harp, song starts,

its protagonist an amateur in such suspect armature
as to even believe in the carefully coupled

emotive substructures of the teenager, these
his and hers antennae attuned to each other

through songs that wed the wishes of its singer
to the limits of his larynx, and in fairness, no

one word isn't already vetted by days and days
of silence. Wouldn't I lay a hand on you, June

a windy sieve of green? Cave art sends its chase
scenes deep into the dark rock. The first poems

recorded only battles. Into the arms of the stranger
who strangles me, I'd scratch your name.

SOLE EVE SPEAKER ADAM SPOKEN TO EVE

First you render it fleeable
    to avoid perfectly innocent
        expression

in an NX 2114 to PS 3551.3
    kind of way.
        Clouds might marble

over, rain warm
    rain.
        A ponderous love,

caught distraught, strikes
    them then as little

        more than elaborate thirst,
evoked only in situ
    or all the fucking time,

        that whole topos
of bimbos the cameras
    hammer and hammer at.

        Adrift in the pixels,
our zero tries and tries

>   to seek but only finds
>   his pictures of the world
> add up to a single weakens

>   for the vulgar sugars
>   of her immediate subject,

as strong in Alexander
>   as apparently it is
>   in astronauts, only so much

more than acetate and light and the expected
>   mimetic, cock pussy cock,

>   puzzling its screens:
in consequence, this
>   constellation cleanly separates

>   posits plain old stars again,
largely the relic of radio
>   singing an aria

>   introducing himself to her

retrenchments, enjoyed
>   in their original tongue.

ON THE LONG-STANDING RELATIONSHIP BETWEEN THE FINGERSNAP AND THE WORDS *LIKE THAT*

At certain speeds these
bridge abutments strobe
the harvest moon,

a flip-book-quick look
of the shamble of a lampshade
of a lifetime. So much

moon in the smoke trees this
road ribboning the river seems
the dirtiest candy on the planet.

It wasn't the child with a magnifying
glass and so much summer
on his hands so much

as its sharpened point of light.
So long, up close. Welcome
to the Wyoming of my eyes

whenever I'm around you.
Next to me a couple studies
osteopathy, textbooks open on

the Fascia of Orbit and Eyeball.
It's the love story of the tragic
evolution of the ductwork

of the tear. Their lettered diagram
ransoms back its random piece
of me—the jelly of an eye, a sleeve

of vein. Small oval clouds
reposition the theme in between
an overriding sense of the over-written

remedies for heartache, and rain,
which keeps the image supple
by an active connection to flux

and frame. The way waking
releases the trees from wherever
they were the second before

I open the blinds. Wind twists
in the grasp of the barbed wire fence,
little nails bent into snarls, and out

amid the nippled apples, another
species of leaf casts the same
dark shadow. The traffic sign

down by the hospital says
Begin One Way, and first appears
to be about beginning.

TRANSCENDENTAL ANCHORAGE

So what the sunset's just more summary
of one whole daylight or another

                         angry paraphrase, as the still lakes
glaze. True, who wants to get into all that darkness again, anyway,
and for what, but truer still is tragedy

                         ain't really a strategy. Look.

Another imaginary Alaska
laid right out over the real one. The closest I'd always come
to any destination was maybe

                         its map. Maybe more and more

phone lines mandolined clouds
into thin enough slices to read through, only what we read
was only what we wrote, and mostly

                         this. Call it commonplacent, a kind
of contentment with the everyday
every single day. Every

                         number in my life's like a four and a nine,

eight eight something, a six, oh five
oh or seven one seven one. There. We know each other
only by a trial

                         of error, either alone amid abundant

twoness or paired and despaired.
There's anyway only ten numbers,
                                    but 26 letters, which comes to almost
three apiece, and that's a word, and sometimes two. The

past outnumbers the present in its many
                                    moods, all its leaf-slowed sun
of ordinary early Junes I dreamed
I was some soluble beach ball, but when I woke

was only late.
I'll allow all of it's soluble, all of us
solvable, our lots and lots of problems,
                                    which itself is only one, so why not?

A cardiologist I once cornered swore
the heart in the hands
                              is like a perfect water balloon, and it's his
job not to get any big ideas.

NO NOTE

First snow powdered onto darkened parks and farms
while I just wanted our prop plane down

                                          in a tightened spiral, I tell you,
of streaming debris, wings
flaking away as my pilot and I perish, half an hour out. I thought
about how I didn't somehow have the coat

                                          for opening my little door,
thumbing the button, turning the red arm clockwise like he'd said,

thought if I could get my foot against his seat,
loop my belt around his neck and with all my weight

                                          lean back—steepening
climb, nose dive—he'd take evasive measures, he'd barrel roll, so
I'd have to hold
on for dear life. I thought

               about the last of the leaves burnt to blue haze about
eleven feet above the street

the day before I left, and how I'd have to keep
at it once the struggle stopped,
because TV

        taught me fake your black out early
enough, then wait for your murderer to tire.
Instead I stared

            and stared at the lasagna of cloud
together we climbed above.

MINE OWN RECOGNIZANCE

To extract libidinal substance
from the losable, which
in its middle is the sea,

just look. As many bathers
as any canvas can handle, yet
worth study also is the single line

that begins at the top of her
back and continues to her toes,
which turns and all along explains

its girl (as Milton's Eve wearing
only her hair). They first teach cops
to tell whether someone broke in

or someone broke out, depending
where the shards are. Winter
sunlight windowed in and we,

sweet pea, we went to pieces.
*Such an enemy we have that
seeks our ruin.* To know this

transience is to arm against
morning. To first learn to walk,
you can forget how to run.

WEATHERMANIC

Every other second somewhere
there's a thunderstorm but here
phone line shadow on a fence
and backyard, both, the latter mostly
smudge and former edged more
finely. It's hard to talk anything
other than weather to others,
while to myself it's light. Right after
storms it's somewhere sideways,
the dark wet, rain weight, single
bead of water, blown glass dome
of sky. The accumulated life
of any cumulus cloud's like ten
minutes, tops, and 200 something
tons, so what? At the window, textbook
weather riffles this letter to whomever.
Whatever wind there is in the flags
shakes with the shape of the day,
which it twists into a sort of slow tornado
that takes all week. First, I had this balloon
to land in the thickets, but for what?
We couldn't figure out a flower,
gramophonic in the short grass.
The real thing, imagine. I guess
I've been conscious of misspelling
conscience, but I'd never let it
bug me. Anyway, onward inched

the denouement, toward bordering on
beginning again. Home snapped
down around me, stock footage
I'd play backwards of all of its walls
popping away in a storm. It's just
months milked of single days
on which I'd almost wake. That was
the winter whenever the heat went on,
whoever was talking was full of shit,
which was the Spring I wouldn't still
shut up. Dusk and dawn obeyed
the same sorbets. Each just upped
its dosage of darkness or light, in skies
the same pale clouds crumbled across.
I could never remember whether
it was the valley of the shadow
or the shadow of the valley, but surely
formulae purl forth for even this
quiet, a pocket of calm blown around
to see which trees the light does what with.

LISTING

*—for Johann Benedict Listing, the unacknowledged
other discoverer of the Mobius strip*

what was on it. He smoothed the crushed
                              paper and read

                    *

  this fallen tree's hull is the sentence. The mites' eaten trail in

                    *

   mountain by mountain
   for hours. The rain arriving
                        erases the range

                    *

in fact changes any thesis. The way
                 dropping to your knees

                    *

      advances and retreats. Take these
                              dispatches about

*

massive trade in breakables. A preponderance
          of shards implies

*

  the world
     is to want to save it. One response to

*

skies they're falling from. Attitude
        also means the way planes are in

*

 eyes they resemble. Then you're picking olives
          because of whose

*

one long leaving. The river in its living glaze is

*

was and would be all along. The thing it was
         back then was

*

    to be a plum blossom
    is a little blood
    in balled-up cellophane.

                          Trash spills across the lawn
                          until what appears

SURVIVAL OF THE FITTING

It's why wanting to miss home
    kept real to me
the faces there. Car tires

    hissed down wet streets,
whispered stay or stray

    or both. There's nothing
to cry about, which always
    chokes me up. Nothing

adds up so much
    as jumps ahead
to equals. The birds

    fill with trees. Short rain
steams on roads the sun
    resumes. I'd said

everything I had to
    and still

there seemed one or two more
    commas left over. It all
just ended.

>   Hot tap water, top hated
> waiters, whatever. Look,
>   you've got to love somebody
>
> or somebody is going to love you.

MINIMUM SECURITY BLANKET

At most we'd give this year's first
attempts at dusk a C/C+. That's just
us. It's getting there, though. It's got to

get later. That's all. There are
no mistakes around here. Only correction.
We might not have a crime, but we got

plenty of bodies. A cloud of blackbirds
lifts and twists its one big thumbprint
snowfall dusts for, its motive

opportunity, its every wound defensive.
Down here in the grain of this engraving
all dots clot into dark and distance, the 16th

Century. So when Herkinbald crunches up
from his deathbed etching to gouge out
the larynx of his rapist nephew—that

open eye socket hold he has of him,
the skull's impression on the pillow
a plug he'll fit back into after—it might be right,

that words can cite but never sight
their object. Yet we'll rub our eyes all
over it a while, walk out of the gallery

blinking the periphery back into being. Ink jet
pixilate, anyone, I, when I go dot dot dot,
I go dot dot dot a lot. There's no way to describe

the dead moths in the streetlamps. And when
any window's one tree makes its moonslaw,
sure, we'll shudder, shouldn't we?

Even if the little shit had it coming, here
it
is.

HOW TO HAND SCISSORS OR KNIVES
TO SOMEONE YOU LIKE

First write the treatise on the causes of the giving
way of walls, then, separately,
                          treat their remedies. Let the uncut mood
clutter up. Let the let down now

                          let down their guard again. Go ahead.
Grind your teeth
away each night then wake first thing to sing, sunlight
a local solvent of years, and yet

                          each day, each minute in it
the old song crumples newly, smoothes
to prose that holds up mirrored
                          sunglasses to nature, out there

where the hibiscus twists its photographs of flowers,
where we laughed best
and last and made the most of the mint, cups of snow
with our Kahlua.

                          Write night stood
opposite, the only prop. Write how it next subsides
in greater collapse, then how it comes to topple.
                                        Then why.

Trouble deepened,
                yet made it safe enough for finally diving
into what the dearest to him persist in
calling my life, the long deep

clear I steered
of everyone. Clouds straight face
                this horizon that wants to bring them all in anyway
for a few routine questions. It's not the name in the airport p.a.

but that someone somewhere's calling.

CINCINNATIA

From the beginning
it's one big middle
threatened with ending

and threaded in
dickhead metaphysics. The soul
a big bowl of coke

and body an armada
of dildos a-thrum. Come
on. The soul's a soapdish

pearling milk down through
its sieve. The soul's as old
as I am. And childhood?

I remember a window
in many of my math classes,
invisible things

the squiggles were
doing to each other again.
I had an idea

for less than one.
I had one about Ohio.
I knew it was for sure

suspicion, but was it
sinking or sneaking? How
Ohio? Oh, you know.

RIVER AS A RAIN MUSEUM

The great subjects continue
to paint the distant heart
partial to synopsis. Injury, help
for it. One one day, another
another. Today the sky is late

ash leaves, hazel and seems
deep elms. Autumn's all
deciduous asides and unrepeatable,
which gives it an aggregate
gravitas, here in the long logo haul

up into daylight. Again I'm a ghost
wrapped in prosciutto, and sit
like a happy man where the river
unwinds its oiled length of rope,
slackens back to Arkansas,

a strip of film, burlap-colored bag
of cats, close to dirt as water gets.
More, then, meets the eye, as day
fills its mob scene soliloquies
with what real there was

to go around. The bed's made
up its mind, the shirt occurred,
a tie, and in swims the Mississippi
in medias res, immediately
restless, quickened with rain

and debris in its creases, a city
aloft at the edge of it. Backlit
pigeons eyelash the smokestacks.
Dead cars hedge the avenues,
as the landscape leafs down.

In the shattered slate of this
riverbank, up trumpet some
late blooms, white weeds
moored between the broken
greens and browns of bottle glass,

the rusty vertebrae of gutted bass
and mackerel. How are two people
to piecemeal even one bite
of a day like this, at once
both open and parenthetical,

moreover November, replete
with red tiled roofs and phone
booths the sun becomes, transitive,
shadow its object, and me
the guy to cast it. Around here

a lot of truth gets pulled over
your eyes, fully woolen.
A certain sooth gets said.
I love you, for instance,
and that's your problem.

ARDOR VITAE

For a long while, link a few littler instants, staple
stab, fender gleam, the simple aspiration of these weeds

in window-colored wind or broken bottle held together
by its label, only by its name in puddles rain zeroes

and zeroes, then cloudbreak and blackbirds blued
by sudden sun. The grasses roll. Lilacs brush the fence

barbs and lilies star a yard, little help with wind
the blades wave onward and along, but then it's still,

and the trees just plants. The trees ring. I'd be fine
with each year's end of summer suffering

us such suffix, if only I knew then what we knew
then. The sky a marble rye a few birds fly, a kind

of caraway, though let's not get carried away
with this vision's pigeons, letter-legged, I beg you.

In wind these leaves aren't the tethered feathers of held
back birds, but another world squinted into, another rouse

to true, screw to loosen, hurt worth a sermon, surely,
but what about the mirth of mumblers under their umbrellas?

So Summer stumbles into what it is, what it's going to
have to have been. We came to the end and kept on

middling. This is how it works. The well-worn
thoughts knot and scram, lump up then evaporate.

I therefore think I am, and follow the fish-shaped shadows
of the almond-shaped leaves of these walnut trees

under which we wonder what to just do. Clouds school.
The sky's blue spools. And that'll do a while. A couple

of cumulonimbus do their humble crumble, at least
stood for something. Anything. Falling, even. Down.

Into this gristle and its bone, this little book of knitted
throws, of antique barbs in which it's not too late,

its Dodge Six Point Stars and Knickerbockers, the Kelly
Thorny Common, the Four Point Twirl on Large Strands,

Twirl on Small, and on and on along the fenced up
wiry skies which wash this grit of stars.

BLACK TERN

To take a petroglyph and retrofit some significance onto it's
easy. It's not *only* know thyself the oracle enjoins, after all,
so I'm out stumbling around Thousand Hills State Park again
to discover one thing turning into another—this boulder,
a plover—because the world offers thought what it becomes.
Rene Magritte, though, thought thought becomes what the world
offers, and also that this guy was a huge rock floating in the sky,
so who am I to scare these terns nesting in the park shelter
shading centuries old symbols scored into sandstone, each
hawk-trough a good inch and a half deep into the rock?
In Summer under the long light of late afternoons, each
hollowed out swallow shape fills with shadow, each tern
extruded by the pooling dark, just regular rock at work at
mold-injecting bird after bird worth of night. The real sense
in which it captures its vulture isn't just a 2-D representation
of it in the sky, but a little machine made to make its shadow
on the ground at your feet, and you're put in mind of highways
sometimes driving into the shadow of an airplane passing overhead.
Next to the next to last of the light gone candy again, the cirrus
clouds seem far off sucrose combing over and away. And under it
this little flock of petroglyphs charts out art's old elemental
alchemy. Simple stone into sky. Go and ask Magritte why
mimesis will always release us from the same old spot we're on
and he's liable to say mystery means nothing either, mister.
So this outcropped rock's a kind of cloud some birds emerge
from, a millennial manila, its color, French vanilla, left out like
eleven hundred years. The stone's so soft it seems you'd only

need a seed to scratch a word or two onto it, so soft a single drop
of rain would make a name for itself there beside *Bonnie,
Ron,* and *Twila* or the *Class of Zero*. Not far away from another
deeply creased crow there's *BJ*, etched in all right angles,
which either indicates the name of yet another engraver
or commemorates some other moment chosen from the recent
past of this place, one the stone sort of enacts with the same
sense of soaring. After all, it's this little sudden give in gravity
it gives, a single frame of flight, a form of fossilized sight.
You can tell these swallows by the cursive of the winglines,
the splits in the tail, a geologic instant fixed, caught mid-careen
in between a really old creek and this violet hum of dusk
up above the lake it's become. Swallows shaping lake mud
into one smooth stone secure their nests in the ceiling beams.
But back at the bird book I want it to be a black tern so bad—
first for the title, then this shit year or two I've been through.
Poor you've really seen a black turn, that sort of thing, but
I'm glad it's not the one a page earlier, 236, the *Least Tern*,
because of that tiny space between the words, its stopped
consonants bitten in two. Even if a struck flint of silence,
of a mouth clamped down's how it flies, however, in quick
trips to the water, the way they boomerang around you here,
part bat, part blow dart. It's a quick glimpse to try to catch,
I'd guess, and etch into this hillside. Drawn—which means
pulled along, as in the first six or seven seconds of a song,
and also *filled,* as in baths and the buoyancy of bodies, and
towards, as in attraction or as two words, drawn *to words*
to ward off silence, a tension attention attends to with its chisels
in this mineral cloud of hammered up dust and such crumbling.

ECHO LOCAL

Just when you think that cloud
is the least thing you'll see
all day, this city tightens
its brick mask, July

revives, gets finally around
to explicating May,
and with any luck
before long June,

because there's so much
around to get to. Back then
survival didn't seem so
liable, its wheel ruts far less

pliable, and there's the road
and where we went right off.
Spring so the whole zone
greened. It was a real bargain.

It didn't cost us everything.
Just a couple of months
composed of soap
and sausage. Part smoke,

part post office boxes. Rain
and maybe the red money
of another country. The chairs
of the place and the songs

of their dragging. Its cirrus
sift the ponderous blue down
onto us obliviatti, ear-budded
all about the outlet mall and legion

hall and in the all-night diner
where it was always that summer
you knew everything maybe one
thing at a time or everything

at once and just forgot that
the later you stay the more
you say to the waitresses
you're fine and good and all

set, thanks, yet the warm-ups
wash in. In this quiet hour
the evening wind is heard
to moan in the hollows of your

face, and what you know,
we all know. The coffee cools,
the ice melts, and the universe
searches for its zero.

DEUS EX MACKINAW
—for Herb Scott

Were we reading elegy out
by the pound, announced
down shadowless aisles

of groceries—all echo,
all aftermath, the cashier's
loudspeaker thing as it

swings there—surely
each observant clerk would
scurry out and back,

an apronful of heads of
lettuce, single cubes
of sugar. It's just hunger

and the whole thing starts
over. Today there's two,
three rooms, tops, left

of the old hotel they're
tearing down. Out here
in this wind the caution

tape's a tethered cursive,
long hand, old schooled,
a seeable thing, saying,

look, name a name
to which loss and lament
operate exclusively as

one component of encoding
such dumb luck to be
in town here where you

once worked, Herb, where the bridge
light lands its glass pastel
on the dark drift of

the Mississippi. The ground's
gone bruisable again,
a day the dirt is

a sort of silver in this remembered
aluminum of Lake Michigan
sun, a late winter afternoon

that the crow song goes
two nails at a time into
silence to hold it together.

THE BOY AND THE RIVER
BETWEEN THE GIRL AND THE SEA

Every river knows no ocean
can't be stolen and given
back as bird baths under thunder
claps. With some wind
it itches into sequins, morning
installing its shimmer
on the surface, chewing its foil.
Dawn's long gone. All it is
is early. You can talk blame
home, but dinner won't be ready.
You put an ad in the *Morning Star*
and can't afford the *Evening Sun*
or put one in the *Evening Sun*
and can't the *Morning Star*, saying
someone buy my goddamn car
so I can leave for good.
Whenever anyone comes to this
river with another, invariably
they end up gesturing across
great distances. Good distance,
we get your point about the burnished
muds in Autumn sunlight, sky-deep
water. Our river bends in and away,
scripts its S to the Cape, though
there's no escape, Missouri more

or less a mess you're in with me,
Illinois an edge to reckon. City
gray opalesces in its sheen of piss
and rain decays into a mist or eases
into fog, a form for which we've
little analog, other than the ordinary
blindnesses of those of us that
not so much as people the place
as person it, as though the wreck
of being someone were the best
next thing. Another day tightens down
around its darkness. A certain man
struggles to esteem, it seems,
himself. He may not want anyone
to turn him into this, me, I
don't give a damn. I tried my failures,
laughed things everyone laughed
about times I talked all the time,
yet what described of it there was—
long moonlight, and so on, downtown
tulips—seemed kind of ruinous to chase.
And was this its way? Name and place
bunch into nearly enough to hide you?
Can opener, morning, sink drip, what?
What are those long nights like? Clouds
go bleeding on the drapes of each
interior. The mirrors, misdirected
by a surplus of signification, cancel

into countless nothing. The window
spun on sun and its outages. Big deal,
dusk just played dawn backwards.
It's still a beginning. It's a start.
As beneath bosc trees, one can stand
and there in the pear light, try
as one might to stand it.

SLIDE GUITAR SUNDAY

Poor Desperate, we don't have time
to spell you right. Today is blue dust
and feelings, meaning little, but well.

Cloud swath light splotch floats this
dishwater light. Most days I write
sunlight when I really should shadow.

The little to say packs up and stays,
backs up to the part about this
laughable bafflement meant

only to screw with you. Boredom
and terror cancel into kick drum
snare, kick drum snare. I hear

in my mind all of these voices,
then words, then music and it breaks
her heart, but that's when she loses

me. This one last month of winter
wobbles like any difficult body.
One wet fence wire slices off

its certain length of sun, platinum
choker, single strand of lightning,
God's loud hair were he there. Look,

we'd all like a little more in the monitors.
There's still the same old sorry to sing.
Woke broke, a little blistered, mostly

miffed and missed her. On each new
branch buds bolt up the sky, rivet
far away rain and the day sizzles past,

blister salve blister salve, hardly half
of all we hoped but twice as much
as nothing.

NOTABLE CAPTURES

No way he figured
he'd suffered
page after page
of Sapphic paraphrase
just to go ahead
and lose her
like this.
Winter branches
dredge the starlight,
as the clause of its
sentence implausibly
falls, impoverishes,
enriches the X
that each of her dresses
possesses. Sweet life
device, these
motifs mostly
coalesce, each elegantly
grasped at. Such
sparsely charged
study of a woman.
Some term come to
with loss. The whole
time fragments
saying hey
when I had hold of her
we stayed put.

IN COMMAND OF IRREGULARS

The half of the path behind us
and half yet ahead, it's said, met
in dark woods where the way was lost.
But you pull up one raw rutabaga
and you're bound to get a bunch
of stuff held together by dirt. You're
bound to get some of us. Leaf shadow
leopard-skins these buildings we're in,
where we only know we've only known
the always little we knew, as per Plato.
At least we know a little bit about
the fight for this place, how it started
at the first site of the school. The Confederate
lieutenant sounds a guy who showed
too soon, drawn out easily and routed
south. We know our town, how it slopes
down and away at its western edges,
so the last of the latest Summer light hits
us flush, and the windows of the courthouse
burnish back a docketful of sunset.
Its limestone softens, lamp posts moisten.
Everything's cast in molten cantaloupe,
a tarnished lightning striking at the speed
of geology until the first bat's bent
on flying Q's into the sky's finely milled
dusk. Last call all we sing are songs
on cyclone-thrown pianos, so it's not like

there's any more dizzy left to get.
In the morning despite whatever we are
about to go through, the sky slides black
to slate, whitens and widens, pinks in
places and a thumbprint smudge of cirrus
turns its murk to pearl.

WHAT I ALWAYS THOUGHT I TAUGHT
THIS TOWN'S SONS ABOUT ITS DAUGHTERS

Remember that kid
who kinda couldn't look
at a combine in a dust cloud
lit with late Autumn

afternoon without wanting
a drink of her water?
And her? She couldn't
ride home in the rain

slow enough. A few
newly white-washed
barns blow empty
pages across this

landscape, or anyway would've
if they weren't already ghost
screens of dead drive-ins,
the undersides of leaves

blinking whole other species
of trees and weeds, and he
and she's just trying to hold on
when every bug smudge

on the windshield seems
someone's initials.
And in truth, very few clouds
precipitate. Little rivers

of sandstone gap the native
grasses—glacial scourge
as all of the geomorphologists
call it, in contrast to the glacial

scour an hour or so west. That
one long planed-down plain
smoothes this crimped and buckled
almanac of upper Mississippi valley

where the soybean fields seem
corroded platinum, the corn torn
between green and orange in rows
above which a cloud of crows

rose, and the whole way out
of town the sunset churns
its burning sherbets, sure,
but sunset's also just where

some pink thing thinks
to claw its way out.
And it's going to make it.
Watch.

TUESDAY CO-ED MINOR CHAMPIONS

Former normal schoolers, tell me,
the damp towel dropped on the bed
doesn't have to dramatize impermanence

alone, now does it? Ain't it also ok or even
something happy like the new late February
light of four, four-fifteen, that golden talc

engravers always talked of getting rich
with, one trophy at a time? Often your best
chance at rescue is staying put. The new

blue tulips equal cups of snow. Each rib
of light through the blinds fills with dust
regardless of just what of his him with her

disturbs. What her words were for shirt,
for instance, hurt here in the heart of it. O
love poem, go home. The street warms

toward morning. Trees leaf without warning.
And still we can't believe it. Just saw
morning a few hours ago and it seemed

fine. Dawn first shakes its pink sheets out,
shrouds the bed it's made in us, but the breakfast
held and here we are, reading the recent discovery:

a pair of skulls that push back the known
age of the human form some hundred-thousand
years. So now we've even less to show

for ourselves. Or more. It's Sunday, and the news
is history. The toast is in crumbs. Nowhere
starts now. But ends here.

ACKNOWLEDGMENTS

I would like to thank the editors of *Born Magazine* for publishing "Notable Captures."

I would like to thank the editors of *DIAGRAM* for publishing "Among the Attributes of a Basically Cruel Man," "Mar," and "Iron-Clad Lullaby."

Without whom, nada: Ander Monson, Bill Olsen, Nancy Eimers, Dean Young, Mary Ruefle, Dobby Gibson, Allegra Blake, Marcel Brouwers, Billy Reynolds, the Carcia's, the D'Agostino's, James Cianciola, Jen Creer, Dereck Daschke, Ed Rogers, Joe Benevento, Obi Nwakanma, Chris Lindley, Franklin Cline, Hena Ahmad, Monica Barron, Barbara Price, Alanna Preussner, Arnie Preussner, Troy Paino, Cole Woodcox, Aaron Fine, Julia DeLancey, Susan Swartwout, Leia Wilson, Brad Smith, Phil Schaefer, Drew Turner, Michael Derby, Ray Holmes, John Hitzel, Rachelle Wales, Shawn Bodden, Mary Po Smith, and again and again, Karen Carcia.

COLOPHON

Text is set in a digital version of Jenson, designed by Robert Slimbach in 1996, and based on the work of punchcutter, printer, and publisher Nicolas Jenson.

JAMES D'AGOSTINO is the author of *Nude With Anything* (New Issues Press). His poems have appeared in *Forklift, Ohio; Conduit; TriQuarterly; Indiana Review; Third Coast*; and elsewhere. He lives in Iowa City and Kirksville, MO, where he directs the BFA Program in Creative Writing at Truman State University.

NEW MICHIGAN PRESS, based in Tucson, Arizona, prints poetry and prose chapbooks, especially work that transcends traditional genre. Together with DIAGRAM, NMP sponsors a yearly chapbook competition.

DIAGRAM, a journal of text, art, and schematic, is published bimonthly at THEDIAGRAM.COM. Periodic print anthologies are available from the New Michigan Press at NEWMICHIGANPRESS.COM/NMP.

www.ingramcontent.com/pod-product-compliance
Lightning Source LLC
Chambersburg PA
CBHW031419040426
42444CB00005B/638